MATTHEW GALBRAITH
ARCANA MANNA

Poems by
MATTHEW GALBRAITH

———⊱⊰———

I AWOKE IN DREAMLAND
Poems from Either Side

BLUESHIFT
Poems from a Universe in Reverse

PARTICLE MAN
Third Book of Poems

ZERO SUM
Poems of Equilibrium

ARCANA MANNA

WATCH THE RIPPLES DANCE

ARCANA MANNA

Kindle Direct Publishing
Seattle, Washington, USA

2nd edition: January 2024, rev. August 2024

ISBN: 9798462219986

Library of Congress Control Number: 2021918505

for Nancy
Amy Sarah Jeremy
Gabby Barry Maddie Zoe

CONTENTS

INTRODUCTION

My last book of poems, *Zero Sum,* was published at the very dawn of the 2020–21 pandemic, so most of these works were composed during sixteen months of home isolation with my wife, Nancy.

Throughout the first months of that era, I had no inclination to write poetry, but sometime in early October 2020, ideas began to flow. Now, in less than a year, I have reached my magic number of thirty poems—an astonishing feat for me, who usually averages less than one per month.

And so I'm happy to present *Arcana Manna,* who's meaning is addressed in the opening title poem. Several motifs are explored herein. One dominant theme appears in the third chapter, "Moon"—a thorough scrutiny of the thoughts that continually recycle through my mind during nightly episodes of early-hour insomnia.

It is noteworthy that GOD appears over a dozen times throughout the book in various incarnations, including a title role in the poem "GOD Has No Name"; then twice as a feminine deity, and once each as the Great Invisible and the ancient YHWH.

Chapters "Sun" and "Shadows" offer an assortment of reflections on the various states of mind I experienced during our months of confinement.

"Ignes Fatui" ("Foolish Fires") contains some of the last poems written for this collection. It features a return to the more idiosyncratic, outré-syntactical style I once employed for many of my earlier poems.

Notes on the 2nd edition:

Soon after publication of the first edition, I began to feel that maybe I had left it out of the barn too soon. Something was off but I couldn't say what. Since publishing my latest collection in February 2023 (*Watch the Ripples Dance*), I have not written one new poem, so I decided to spend some time revising a few things in previous books and declare them to be "Final Editions." I saved this one for last, as I knew it would require a lot of extra work.

As it turned out, 20 poems were still good as is, six required a few enhancements, two required major surgery ("Doors" and "Sleepy Thoughts"), one was eliminated altogether, and the title poem, "Arcana Manna," is a total rewrite—doesn't even remotely resemble the original. I also designed a brand new cover!

I'm quite happy now, and must ask those few folks who own the first edition to please recycle (or burn) the paper and pretend this is a brand new book.

— MG

PROLOGUE

Arcana Manna

Nothingness precedes our fourteen
   billion years of cosmic history
      in which as primates yes we've learned a lot
        but sadly falling short of final truths
      to never be revealed

Like actually what is nothingness?
   Or what are really quarks electrons
      matter energy and all the rest?
        Or evolution toward what end?
         Or depth extent and meaning of our
          mystic consciousness?

But all at very least we know
   that once upon a not so long ago
      on this just one of maybe forty
        billion billion living planets of the universe
          a special child was born somewhere called
            Bethlehem on Earth in the Milky Way
          sent from the depths of the most impossible
        arcane mind of GOD
      to live teach heal suffer die
   and somehow let us know that Love
is all we really need to know

Or plus the deeply joyous freedom
   humbly yes just one of countless
      cosmic creatures writing poems
        that nonetheless are all my own
          sent as manna from the heavens
           drifting through my brain and never
        really meant to sell
      but happy and fulfilled I am
   to make them real
on creamy colored leafs herein

SUN

A Poem With Strangers

My heart's flames rise above
The ubiquitous ether of orbiting orbs
Boiling rocks and frozen gases
And only the stars truly understand
Reaching out through light-years of spacetime
With nourishing rays and the truth of life's beginning

My heart's passions love and hate mankind
From saints to psychopaths
Heroes to sycophants
Artists to horses-asses
The differential chasm is just too much to bear
"Forgive them as you are forgiven" I am taught
But mostly I just can't

In the witching hours of hopelessness
In passive semiconsciousness
I meditate compose and float
My phantom wordless prayers to the Great Invisible
Then deep within that formless haze
Sometimes I see more clearly
Veins of insight hidden by the light

And so I'd like to write a poem with strangers
Scribing unpremeditated verses
On bare white walls in an empty room
With folks who shall remain unnamed
Then go our separate ways

I See You

I see you but I don't understand you
Ten years old with bare stems halfway up
Standing tall through brown stubs of past generations
A quiet village of leafage and then
Six canary yellow roses!
Out in the pure blue sky and chill of mid-October

We share the same orbit you and I
Same air and calendar of seasons
I found you in a nursery
Lifted you up and brought you home
Tilled my garden thoroughly
Laid you in the ground just so
Watered you and watched you grow

Every year I mark your certain arc
Of rebirth life and death
A silent steadfast friend and yet
A stranger in a stranger world
I fail to know you truly as I fail to know myself

But in this breath of reverie I now begin to see
We're only different shapes and shades of the universal ONE
And through these countless nights and days
We rest our fates in the cupped invisible hands of Mother GOD

Cicadas

Cicadas serenade the end of summer
But in my ears they sing the whole year round
Roses spike the wayward hands
But spiteful thorns pierce my age-worn shoulders
Long into the night and every waking hour

But I don't complain as my eyes can see
Colors far outside the rainbow spectrum
My skin can sense each molecule of shrouding atmosphere
I taste the fruits and breathe the pristine scents
Of virgin forests in my secret thoughts

My ears can hear Earth's music in every seething atom
The whispers and the rages of her bio-machinations
The terrifying flames and flashing rays
Of the never-ending turnings of the cosmos

And my chorus of cicadas and prickly rose bouquets
Abide with me through each enchanted day
As vigilant sentinels and faithful companions
Sharing every pulse of my awareness

GOD Has No Name

GOD has no name or voice we can hear
No he she or it
Form mind or substance
We can feel GOD in stillness and silence
In a certain kind of sadness or abandon

Prayers need no words
Although words soar highest in prayers
Words are mere symbols for deeper realities
Vapors arising from ultimate truths
That elude the blunt tools of language and reason

Primary particles can't exist
Without interactions with other particles
Neither can love stand alone in a vacuum
It thrives in continuums of conscious beings
Flowing from mind through mind and heart through heart

Love has no mass or energy
Electrons gluons or quarks
And how much more meaningful would love be
If we didn't call it "love"?

The heat and light from the Sun
Spectral rays of stars
Cool reflections floating out from the Moon
And all the miracles of life on Earth
Assimilated all together
Would seem more wondrous if they had no names

And so I'll say goodbye to "GOD"
(Although poets are artists who paint with words)
And say hello to whatever

Once

Once
In a chair
In an unlit room
In solitude
In stillness
In a prayer
I saw GOD's hand reach through the darkness
To rescue me
To grasp my hand
And all I had to do was ask

Invisible Dance

Free from the millstone of gravity
And tether of primate constraints
Nature's invisible dance was tranced
In the stars' imaginations
At the dawn of creation

Sowing spacetime throughout the cosmos
They ideated music in clouds of dreams
Beaming life to the unborn forms
Of future sentient beings

Then pulled aground by jealous gravity
And tangled in the viscera of planets
Our animated limbs and muscles
Nonetheless arose to move and flow
In concert with our praising voices chanting to the sky
In modal rounds from pastures tents and temples

Quite an enlightening moment of joy
To surrender with impulse and passion
Arousing our tired and fearful hearts
Suspending our bewilderment
And shading our natural blues into phrases of motion

White

I think it may be apropos
In a virgin winter snow
To compose an ode to white

I'm not talking about the debutante's gown
Or her Georgia peach Caucasian skin
But luscious clouds in a depth of azure
The ivory orbs of your lover's eyes
Black pupils jade irises gleaming

White is the queen of the primary palette
The lowest entropy one can imagine
A rainbow bouquet of cosmic waves
Shot backwards through a prism
The antidote for a crippling funk
The essence of patience and guardian of balance
The one load of laundry I do with hot water
The disturbing voice of your conscience

And white and black are a perfect marriage
They canter all through the town and the roundabout square
Swinging smoldering thuribles wafting through spacetime
On black and white horses brushed and adorned
With tresses woven in ribbons of silver and gold

Then white can stand alone in black
In the absence of matter and energy
Dispersed into ultimate nothingness
Ready to spawn a new universe
In a birthing rainbow blast

MOON

Chasing Twilight

I know there's magic in that special place
The fertile seam that floats between
Our waking and the catacombs of dreams
For me to reap its rare and potent essence
Elusive as horizon's edge
That's why I'm chasing twilight

Translucent spirits rise from blooming dreamscapes
Drifting in and out of my fading consciousness
Like leprechauns or mesons
To flash the keys to impervious koans

Words and phrases formed in full awareness
Sift through the veil to the other side
Swirl through the air in otherworldly scenes
Diffusing and devolving into babble

A secret portal opens in the rising Moon
I swim toward its light
The looming shade of sleep is closing in
One more micro-breath remains
For me to snatch the charms and spells of twilight

Night

Night is Creation's daughter
And in the still of Dylan's owl-light
Makes it known that she
Is so much more than absence of the Sun
Or a shroud of grounded clouds

And Night is a passive teacher
A sober equalizer
Who dissipates the lies of day
Mutes emoting colors
Sketching truths in simple black and white

And deep within her sheltering womb
She paints my room in silken darkness
Charms the air with the music of silence
Conjured from the deep sea's mysteries
And tuned in the quiet peace of a solitary chapel

And when I offer up my soul
With sorrowful abandon
She distracts me momentarily
Slides her needle stealthily between my glassy eyes
And waits with me until I fall asleep

In a Dark Room

In a dark room
Stripped bare of daylight's deceptive images
On a planet spinning thoughtlessly in unrelenting circles
I try to visualize or imagine truth
To feel it in my honest heart

To peel away layers of human knowledge
Macro down through micro
Sifting through all the wisdom of science
Philosophy and theology
Resting in right mindfulness
Meditation and prayer
But truth is nowhere I can touch or see

Then faith is all that's left
Standing on a sea cliff
Out at the perilous ledge
Legs trembling
Chest tight with fear
Gazing out across the magnificent ocean
Birds and blue sky
Trusting mute and formless GOD
To catch my fall

Regret

It's going to keep me awake I fear
It's starting to look that way
That throbbing toothache
Snake in the outhouse
Shiv in the belly
Demon Regret

Like a low-lying unmanned island at night
In the rushing Amazon River
Brooding alone in the three o'clock gloom
Guilty as sin with no one or nothing to blame
Assessing the loss of a friendship of forty years
Accepting the fate of my self-destructive mistake
I lie staring up at the ceiling
Waiting for those two little pills
To wipe my memory clean
And bludgeon me to sleep

Moon

Sleepy Thoughts

Sleepy thoughts of random nonsense float by like litter
On the surface of my shallow stream of consciousness
As lying on the silty river bed
Gazing upward through the flotsam
I await sleep at 4AM
When wider deeper darker waters soon emerge
To carry me away through lost and lonely dreams

Water is deeper than merely nature
As dreamscapes with casts of strangers appear
In visitations from faraway galaxies
Of yet unborn realities

Once in a dream I was swimming a wide wide river
At night near the city lights and I had no fear
Gently floating downstream limp and credulous
Pondering ancient truths like the doctrine of emptiness

But I am not an empty vessel!
No anomalous lump in some quantum field
My name is Matt and I exist!
Even as the restless universal energy
Flows through my singular mind
Then passes on through spacetime
To other worlds in GOD's imagination

And in this fleeting moment's breath
Floating free in spaciousness
My mind and spirit harbor Love
As the highest noble truth

People's Faces

A boundless multitude of people's faces
Showered down from fertile clouds
To the water's edge of human history
To soak the seeds of their own beginnings

Spawned and hatched in the streams of nothingness
Spewed in a flash as ghosts across the nascent universe
They drifted lost for eons in the cold flaming Astral Sea
In search of form and substance and a place called Home

And so one night I was lying out
On the cooling sand by the seashore
Trancing up through the Milky Way
When suddenly the sky was filled
With a legion of people's faces
Raining down like the Fourth of July
Like cosmic immigrants crashing the Wall
And bobbing up and down in the surf
In a laughing siege of freedom

Then the world at once turned black
And the people's faces ebbed away
But reappeared quite suddenly
As angel choirs in the sky of my midnight dream

Doors

I dreamed a house with doors in every wall
   and each door leads to another room of
      doors—then I have to choose

And other folks appear in the rooms
   plus cats and dogs all passing through
      in search of just one room with a window
         or a door to the blessed outdoors
            where the Sun shines down

Then I woke in a sleeping walk
   with the aura of the dream still lingering
      to the end of the hall and entered a door
         to a room I had never seen
            dimly lit in a ghostly blue
               with a skylight and a star shining through
               and a stairway up to the roof

Out in the balmy midnight air
   I stood at the edge of a parapet
      and gazed up through the sky at the Hubble galaxies
         then as I fell with my arms spread wide
            I felt no fear and a peace that is everlasting
            as a gentle hand returned me to my bed

I woke with the sound of rain and faraway thunder
   lying on my back with my hands across my chest
      quietly serene and filled with gratitude and wonder
         for the eerie nighttime interlude
            through the secret doors of my dreams

Fractured Reverie

The stalks chaff grains and harvest scythe
Repeat each year the simple metaphor
We seldom pause to contemplate

Or grapes that burst with juice in the vine
Then crushed by the vintner's press
Recycle endlessly the common tale

We never learn the ending
As we fade into the soporific deep

A rude blink of consciousness
Interrupts a timeless night
Of phantom dreams forgotten
Shrouds me in a cubic cell of darkness
Alone in confusion and fear
Arising fumbling past the furniture
Blind on my animal's trek to the urine bowl
Then back to bed now fully awake
Cycling yesterday's dreary news
And unforgiven mistakes

Three more hours remain
Nothing left to do but pray
To silent GOD unseen

SHADOWS

Election Eve 2020

My slender tree of life bends today in winds of fear
As subterranean warriors
Snaking up through the cold earth of November
Bold naked and shameless
From the sulfurous halls of Hell
Assemble here in open daylight
Ushering in this woeful Age of Darkness

Angry vulgar plebeian hordes waving guns and flags
Gather in vaulted arenas and asphalt lots
Snarling smug complacent slogans
Senza face masks spit flying everywhere
Snarky limp-dick curled-lip pundits
Fan the flames of hate through the radio waves

In the eerie COVID silence
I lie in bed and pray
For brotherhood and unity
As our star-crossed ship America
Sinks through the Sea of Enmity
To the lonely forgotten depths of human history

So Tired

Holy Mother I'm so tired
But not ready to surrender
Still full in heart with centuries of dreams
A fertile mind and so much love to share

But I am old and every night
I lie awake and stare through the ashen mist
As formless figures pantomime my naked fears and sorrows
In a postlude dance to another passing day

And then I pray:

O GOD of transient life eternal
Hear the prayers of your hapless children
Glow your Moon that our ship of fools
Might sail out through the starry midnight blue
And safely come to rest on your gentle shore

Shadows

How many creatures are hidden from the Sun?
Inseminated heifers and neutered calves
Mewling kittens and yelping pups
Jealous runts of an unholy litter
Children of the corn with an angry god

So many gulled sheep are herded into churches
With white-washed steeples piercing the sky
Suckling the pap of clean-shaven preachers
Then drowning their blues in buckets of chicken and slaw

Jesus wasn't a Capricorn
Or the cousin of Santa Claus
Or a firebrand of violent insurrection
He taught us all about love then died on a cross

How many Christians does it take
To simply "love thy neighbor"
Or "judge not lest ye be judged"?
So many believers still living in shadows
Hidden from the Son!

The Sibyl

I asked the sibyl what to say
Of day and night
Good and evil
Snow steam or rain?

"In the deep of heaven's countless stars the closest one floats
obscured from the West over Asian skies where yin and yang
swirl and dance in ghostly fields of energy and water's restless
trinity compels the lifeless minerals to animate all plants and
animals"

Or what to say
Of air land and sea
Tragedy and comedy
Necessity and creativity?

"Formless fathomless oceans cradled by steadfast sands in
concert with the laughing Sun or piercing needles of icy gales
fill the void with music as our struggles for survival interwoven
seamlessly with frontiers of imagination oscillate and ripple
through the memory of spacetime"

Or GOD
Undefinable and nameless
Silent and intangible
Omnipresent or aloof creator?

"Accessible in prayer and meditation [and the cruelty of Nature
notwithstanding] behind before within our eyes YHWH's breath
resides with every pulsing quanta baby's face or tender loving
heart—that when we reach our voyage's end our travel-weary
pilgrim souls shall prostrate low in child's pose and awaiting..."

Year of the Crow

Change happens from within
Not superficially
So now it's her turn
High up in the aerie
Hatching a new reality

And so the road turns
Headlong toward the dense dark forest
Our safe ground quakes as plates shift far below us
And suddenly normality
Fades away in the rear view mirror
We've already had this conversation
Yet we never learn

Then that's when faith returns
There's only one path we should follow
The Sun may rise then disappear
But the true Light shines within us
And as we share our grace with one another
The eerie sheen of the black crow's feathers
Guides our souls up through the trees
To a peace of mind that glows forever

IGNES FATUI

Ode for Alice

In heartfelt moments speaking out
    this secret oath of ode for Alice
        via dithering heights with words
            me feckless rise and fall
                in reverie one afternoon
                    of rain and deep reflections
                        bathed in bright green birds and deeply
                    singing leaves of spring
                must I persevere this queer
            siesta haze procrastination
        thanking some unknown for more
    to follow verses soon

Floating over undertows
    of spooky quantum fields
        now fully dazed in headlamp deer nonplusity
            idly seized in rose aromas
                higgledy-piggledy shapes and moody hues
                    persistently woodpecker head-banging up in
                tree bark self-absorbed
            forest chorus all atwitter
        here and far or nesting unawares
    I cram this pulsing panorama deep inside my face
as lightening pops and sparks across my sensory nerves

    Solemn Solomon Sun quite-a-sudden blazes boldly down
        through gliding hawks in swirling mountain breezes
            color-casting laser beams
                to pining mobs of adulating trees
            now supernaturally in sync
        with everything in everywhere
    including me distinctly mooning planet-eyed:
O how and such the wonder of it all!

Ode to You
for Nancy

Beneath the stars is actually within them
And yes they're fiery stout fantasia
Yes they're gaseous cosmologically
Bold but so are You

Below the stratosphere a dizzy
Height above the vast minutiae circus
Stirs a wind of once a lifetime
Only one of Me and all of You

And so I yes I
Love to hold your
Face within my humble hands
Inhale your Luna gaze into my
Chest incomprehensibly
And sing your radiant heart!

Ignes Fatui

Mostly Now

Mostly now asleep one summer afternoon
May I perceive we clearly dwell
Within the skull and mind

Face and eyes regard and greet the world
Body moves from place to place
Breathes feeds manipulates
While struggling we our flickering mortality
To mitigate all hopeless gravity and entropy

Ergo fast and fleeting thus
And so most earnestly
Immersed in music art and poetry
Joyfully in love with likewise children of the Sun
Spiraling through the Milky Way a whirling Sufi dance
So far as long as GOD may humbly we
Celebrate our life with grace and luminosity!

When I Was a Boy

When I was a boy I loved the rain
Thunder lightning all night long
Wish it never ends
Or crickets loud as you please
Or wind makes the trees swish and sway
Then blows everything away
Or sometimes only quiet and still
With lonely hoo-ing trains a far off mile
Alone in the dark and free with all my thoughts
Who and what could ever better?

When I was a boy I loved a girl
Followed by another one and two
Her hair voice smell skin so soft
And kiss her tender lips
So exciting I'll not forget!
She wears my friendship ring and letter sweater
Hold each other close at the dance
Perfume spells me in a trance
Kiss her tender lips in the gym
So exciting I'll not forget!

When I was a boy my life the world was so alive!
With school and books and sports and friends
Crowded chatter up and down the halls
Radios with baseball games and rock-and-roll
Crisp fresh autumn air and odors up in the bleachers
Public pools and movies cost a quarter
Free to roam the woods and streets all summer
Endless rounds of basketball in the park
Or softball out in the farmer's field
Endless laughing with my friends
I wish it never ends!

Ignes Fatui

Then at once I was a man
And happy finally now with all that also
Joyful most to write my poems
Laugh loving with my wife
Her music always in my ears
Still remember yet all fear and failure
Dark hopeless days mistakes so tragic
(Who on Earth most surely does or doesn't?)

And so and on it goes
Thankfully we pause to kneel and pray
Then looking up ahead the road
And sadly now to knowing:
Some day yes it ever ends

Summons to a Prayer

I can't I must to burst emote
  with weeping or elation
    while inside all around are burning
      forests stars and rages also
        all we see or know but never fully understand
          to hate love ache desire while
            fearing all in one

We half awake yet daylight busy
  cascade words voluminously
    steering from the cockloft
      up and down the day clock
        then sink to sleep in midnight's weird and
          anesthetic womb
            while sadly in a waking dream
              aboard this reckless downhill train
            blind and undiscerning toward its
          hexed and doe-eyed passengers
        we racing toward pure nothingness
      or a once and promised Light

So they whom we call Heart
  now pulses deep within me
    surging the living Blood who urges
      me to stand and face the darkness
        plaguing all humanity
          and rocket fuel across the sky
            this plaintive prayer for mercy
              for you and boldly me

Then back to Earth so thankfully
  for water food and sunlight
    each day awash in air and brilliant colors
      I hope or wish or need but cannot say
        how gracious to my soul our gift of Love!

Ignes Fatui

POSTLUDE

No Words

I can't find words for how I feel right now
And maybe that's a good thing
Something off the menu
Or maybe really nothing

There's a place we may not know
Veiled behind our resting eyes
A neutral site of balance
Recondite in plain sight
Not an insight necessarily
Just a nameless presence in our minds

Somewhere in the sphere of cosmic Love
Or momentary perfect trust in GOD
Or self-acceptance and forgiveness
A prelude to a prayer
Or perhaps it is the prayer

But unto you who's reading this
My secret sense arouses me
To wish you peace and happiness
And share this rare tranquility
With you my unknown friend

Love in Real Time

Goodbyes are all contextual and relative

Goodbyes with all our past friends and lovers
Burn and freeze the heart
And lock the gears of spacetime in our minds

But fertile decades reel on by regardlessly
Relentlessly through each our time-lapse histories

Now standing on the green high hill of mellow age
Looking back along the path
I remember each of them with purest love
And no regrets
And even as we change continually then pass away
All are gathered here this day
Around the evening fire in real time
Very much alive and not forgotten

In the Garden

In the garden pinching weeds extracting roots and all
(Yet to each I must apologize)
Then pulverizing clumps of dirt
My hands spoon an apt recess
Precisely placing roots and plant with cool refreshing water
Enfolding firmly back to Earth her long awaited home

Far afield the worlds churn
In greed predation hate and violence
All is hopelessness
Faith love and empathy labor for light and breath
The cosmos spirals expands and burns
Birth life and death flow seamlessly

But in the garden
Soil flowing through my hands
Roots of flowers safely swathed
Soaked in common water
Time smiles and steps aside
In deference to Now

ABOUT THE AUTHOR

Matthew Galbraith (b. February 7, 1949) grew up in McDonald, Pennsylvania, a small town west of Pittsburgh. He began writing poems in his late teens and occasionally printed small volumes, which he distributed among family and friends. In 2000, he began a ten-year hiatus from writing to engage in an obsessive study of the life and poetry of Dylan Thomas. Other influences include the poems of William Blake, Emily Dickinson, E. E. Cummings, and Leonard Cohen.

Matthew briefly attended West Virginia University (1967–69) and majored in English literature before dropping out to immerse himself in the cultural revolution of the Vietnam War era. Traveling extensively throughout North America, he took on a variety of jobs in disparate places, working as a yacht club laborer in Rhode Island; a Goodwill clerk in Cambridge; an orange picker in Florida; a pea picker in Delaware; a bicycle messenger in San Francisco; and an orderly, dairy worker, and carpenter in West Virginia.

In 1974, he married Nancy Riddle, a graduate student in music composition at WVU. The couple moved to Pittsburgh, where they raised their two daughters, Amy Moontide and Sarah Rose. Nancy Galbraith is now a successful composer and Professor of Composition at Carnegie Mellon University.

After marrying, Galbraith earned a living as a structural draftsman and designer. For the past three decades, he has worked as his wife's manager, web designer, recording producer, promoter, archivist, and most devoted fan.

Galbraith has been an active member of the Lutheran church in Pittsburgh for nearly 50 years, having served on councils and committies, and as a Sunday school teacher, tenor in the choir, guitarist, and web designer. He equally honors all faiths and other points of view.

Made in the USA
Columbia, SC
10 September 2024

41746799R00038